# Since Forty Years Ago

## by Forrest Crissey

An account of the origin and growth
of Chicago and its *First Department
Store* The story of centralized
shopping under one roof
*Its* unique location and
events connected
with its History

Privately printed and presented
*by* THE FAIR · STATE · ADAMS & DEARBORN
in commemoration of its 40th Anniversary

*E. J. Lehmann*

The founder of THE FAIR, was born on January 27, 1849, in
Tetrow, Mecklenburg-Schwerin, Germany. He came to America
in 1858 and his parents established a home in Chicago. Here he
attended school and received religious instruction in the German
Lutheran Church. He died in Chicago on January 4, 1900.

# Since Forty Years Ago

WHAT swift and wonderful changes, what a world of activity, what a marvelous labor of city building, what an unparalleled development of business and social life have been witnessed in this city of ours since forty years ago!

Magic is the only word for the making of a city like Chicago that has transformed from a feeble trading post to a mighty metropolis within the span of a single century, and from a town of small stores to a retail metropolis within a period of two-score years.

How all this happened is one of the most fascinating stories that could possibly be told. It crowds within one human lifetime almost the complete epic of civilization. What a marvelous movie film is the mind of the man or woman who happened to be born in Chicago when it was a sprawling pioneer village and has lived to see it become America's second city! And many an "Old Settler" in Chicago has personally spanned the great gap between these two extremes and seen every step of this development. What film feature ever thrown upon the screen can compare in scope and vividness with such a memory reel? None.

Every shifting of scene drives home the fact that Business and not War is the great Writer of History. Battles may decide the boundaries between countries on the map, but Commerce is the great chemist that fuses many and strange peoples into new and united nations; it is the hand that moves the hands of the war-

FORT DEARBORN, 1857          *Courtesy of the Chicago Historical Society*

makers; it is the power that pushes pioneers into trackless wildernesses and that breaks the trails for the finer things that follow.

There is no place in the world where this process has been so swiftly, so splendidly demonstrated as in Chicago's down-town district. This has been the proving ground for many of the greatest merchandising ideas that the world has yet known.

First look at the way in which Civilization was here crystallized out of Savagery.

A log cabin standing on the point of land where the Chicago River flows into the lake is the first link between barbarism and civilization, the earliest symbol of Commerce, for it shelters the French trader, Le Mai, and his squaw wife.

Next comes Government and Trade traveling almost by the same boat — for in 1803 Captain Whistler of the United States Army, his son, Lieutenant William Whistler, and their wives, together with a small company of soldiers arrive for the building of the first Fort Dearborn, followed in the Spring by John Kinzie, an adventurous silversmith who desired to become an Indian trader. Kinzie brought his courageous wife and her daughter by a former husband. Kinzie found profitable employment for his skill in making silver trinkets to catch the fancy of the Indians and pots and kettles of copper for their use. Here was the foundation of Manufacture and Fine Arts. The Kinzie cabin stood on the ground now occupied by Kirk's Soap Factory.

Now we come to the important fact that when once Trade strikes a taproot into the soil it is generally there

THE FAIR IN 1875

to stay. You may destroy every sign of Commerce from the place where it has been planted, and say: "This spot is not for Trade:" But return after a little and you will find that your edict has been mocked, that Trade has sprung up from that soil like thistles and that Business cannot be banished from any place where the atmosphere of natural Opportunity is favorable to its growth.

The fate of the settlement that grew up about the first Fort Dearborn teaches this lesson with a tragic vividness. In a single day it was completely wiped out. That was when the War of 1812 terrorized the country. The Indians massacred most of the soldiers and settlers, captured a few and scattered the remainder. The fort

THE SAUGANASH TAVERN              *Courtesy of the Chicago Historical Society*

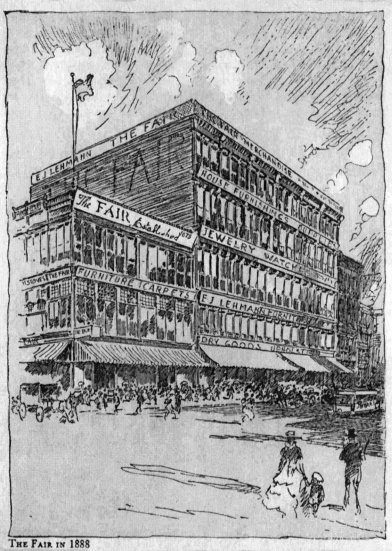

THE FAIR IN 1888

was burned and Barbarism shouted to Civilization and Commerce: "You are as dead here as if the face of a white man had never been seen on these shores." But in four years, the government having re-established the fort, Trade was back at its pioneer task. Kinzie the Silversmith was again on the ground in his old cabin with his brave wife and children — plying his clever hammer. It was almost as if Destiny had lifted a warning hand and declared:

"I have set this place apart for Trade. Neither fire nor sword shall prevail against it. I have decreed that here Business shall work its wonders. Commerce, not the Indian medicine man, shall here develop its mighty magic. This spot, now desolate and in ashes, is forever dedicated as a perpetual proving ground for the greatest principles of Modern Merchandising."

THE FIRST COURT HOUSE AND JAIL    *Courtesy of the Chicago Historical Society*

One of the next important steps in the development of this new civilization was the coming of a black-smith, in 1823. The advent of David McKee was hailed with delight by the settlers of the whole country. He set up his anvil and bellows in a little log shop where the old Wells Street Station of the Chicago and North-western Railroad formerly stood. The mending of traps, guns and tools and the making of many forms of implements gave this first smithy his main occupation.

What most concerned these rebuilders of this wonder-ful outpost of Trade was the re-establishment of those beginnings of Business that the Indians thought they had wiped out in the massacre of 1812. One by one, the elements necessary to make the little community more and more self-sustaining were welcomed. It was

THE FIRST POST OFFICE                    *Courtesy of the Chicago Historical Society*

a big day for the settlement when it gained its first harness-maker on May 29, 1833, in the person of Silas B. Cobb, afterwards one of Chicago's millionaires. His shop was on the spot designated in an early Chicago directory as 171 Lake Street. Then the opening of its first butcher shop and slaughtering house, in 1827, by Archibald Clybourn, marked the beginning of the great meat industry in Chicago.

No doubt the opening of the first millinery shop in the settlement by Mrs. Abram Gale, in 1835, was one of the most significant steps in the evolution of this great Trade center. A community whose commerce can be conducted without a millinery store is certainly not high in the scale of civilization. Perhaps it is hardly too much to say that society—in the more formal sense of the term, at least— began in Chicago with the opening of this unpretentious shop on Lake Street between Wells and LaSalle Streets, as described in present-day terms.

From the viewpoint of the present, the opening of a little millinery shop in a log cabin seems almost a trifling matter. But it was far from that. It stands in the business history of Chicago as her first step in distinctly feminine trade. Subtract from Chicago's commerce of to-day that part of it depending wholly upon women and the reduction would be appalling.

But in these pictures of the processes by which Trade transforms a savage wilderness into a wonder-city, we must not overlook the first tavern, the first school, and the first church. These are named, not in the order of their importance, but of their coming.

When Mark Beaubien came in 1826 and soon opened to the public the cabin from which his famous Sauga-

HOUSEFURNISHING DEPARTMENT

nash tavern was later constructed, the term "down town" took on a new definition; thereafter "down town" stood for the tavern where the genial Frenchman met all comers and made them welcome to the settlement. But the capacity of this tavern was limited, and as the influx of settlers and transients increased, the Green Tree was built, and the borders of "down town" were once more broadened.

The civic center of the Thirties was really the forks, where the Post Office with the Sauganash, Wolf and Miller taverns on their respective sides of the Y-shaped river, constituted the down town. And it is from that Y-shaped junction that the present emblem of Chicago has been derived.

Naturally the whole social life of the young community centered in the taverns where the news from the outside world was first received, where each prairie schooner from Indiana or from "Egypt" or from back East halted and where all the dances and gala events of the embryo city were held. Almost it might have been said that Chicago had no "down town" until her first tavern opened its hospitable doors.

STATE STREET ENTRANCE

Education came early to the little settlement. In 1816 a discharged soldier taught some eight or ten pupils in a little cabin in the Kinzie garden. Later, Miss Eliza Chappell opened another log-cabin school on the southwest corner of State and South Water Streets. It was not until 1833, however, that a public school was established and started with an attendance of twenty-five pupils. At last Trade had obtained so firm a foot-hold that she could plant the seeds of Education and provide for their cultivation.

A new and distinct flavor was injected into the ever-broadening meaning of the homely phrase "down town" when, in the early Thirties, the first churches were organized and three houses of worship erected. Can you not realize something of what that meant to the pioneer women who had not been inside a church for many years and who hungered for some of the refinements and formalities of life as only a woman's heart can hunger after years of exile in the wilderness? No great amount of either imagination or piety is necessary to picture the throbs of excitement with which

ADAMS STREET ENTRANCE

those pioneer women who had braved the long period of churchless Sabbaths, put on their modest finery and prepared to walk down the aisles and take their places in the family pews for the first time. Dressing for the dances at the taverns was tame compared with the novelty of "getting ready for church."

And this is how the spirit of Trade planted civilization in the wilderness where Chicago now stands and started the great stream of Commerce that has been swelling to greater proportions with each succeeding year. As late as 1832 Chicago's first frame store building was put up and her first Post Office was established only the year preceding that. Perhaps nothing suggests the wonderful swiftness of Chicago's development to its "more than two millions" quite so graphically as the simple statement that the first high school here was opened just fifty-nine years ago. Only eighty-two years ago, in 1833, the first "town board" of the village of Chicago was elected and Thomas J. V. Owen was named as its President.

DEARBORN STREET ENTRANCE

While Chicago incorporated as a city in 1837, and elected William B. Ogden as its first Mayor, it was really a trading town, a sprawling village as late as the early Forties.

Furniture Department

From a certain day in 1833 when the schooner NAPOLEON sailed out of the harbor with Chicago's first export shipment of native products, the Wholesale Period of her trade began. True, great fortunes and reputations were made in retailing during that time, but the emphasis of development was along wholesale lines. Brilliant history was made in wholesale methods in that era, and wonderful work was done in developing a sound credit and sales system. However, few new, important, or original ideas in retailing were developed in this time. Growth in the retail field followed along conventional lines until 1875 when a new force entered the retail arena so quietly that its presence was scarcely noticed until it had gathered a momentum that carried it on from an obscure beginning to a marvelous success.

This force was the principle of CENTRALIZED SHOPPING, of RETAIL MERCHANDISING FOR THE MILLIONS, instead of for the few. It embodied the Down Town Spirit as nothing before it had ever embodied it.

It was just forty years ago when E. J. Lehmann founded THE FAIR. This event was so big with commercial consequences that it is worthy of a far greater celebration than the issuance of this historical monograph; it might well be generally memorialized by the whole merchandising world.

Did E. J. Lehmann recognize his plan as a great PRINCIPLE? Did he see it as one of the greatest merchandising discoveries thus far brought to light? I doubt it. So far as I am able to learn from those who knew him personally, he simply had a shrewd idea that he had hit upon a scheme that would "draw trade down town." But if a man with the far-reaching vision of

JEWELRY DEPARTMENT

a Moses had said to him: "This will bring you millions," he would probably have laughed at that prophecy as an extravagant joke. Really he was opening up an ocean of wealth when he thought that he was merely tapping a barrel of "good business."

But just what was it that Mr. Lehmann discovered that revolutionized the whole history of Retailing?

Everything for Everybody under one roof, at a lower price — and that price an odd price. Here you have the whole thing crammed into a nutshell.

He saw the immense economic strength of sheer VOLUME.

The broken nickel price was a brilliant novelty that made a marvelous appeal to the people. The chance to "save the odd cents" was an allurement that went straight to the thrift of the frugal housewife who had been raised upon the sound and ancient economic doctrine "Look out for the Pennies and the Dimes will take care of themselves."

The housewife reasoned well when she said to herself: "Here is an article that cost a store five cents. And because it has never been fashionable for a storekeeper to break a nickel he charges ten cents — an advance of a hundred percent — for it. But THE FAIR asks only seven cents. It is less afraid to break a nickel and a precedent than to take a toll of a hundred percent profit."

In combination the two ideas—Everything for Everybody under one roof and the odd-penny bargain price — seemed to work a veritable miracle and make the currents of retail trade turn about and flow upstream. They

GROCERY AND MEAT DEPARTMENT

put competition into retail buying and transformed family shopping into a high adventure.

The genius of Mr. Lehmann's idea lay in the fact that he recognized this trait of human nature and saw the extent to which it could be used to *move trade* to *centralize shopping.* He was himself a poor man and this circumstance put him in position to realize the problems of the people, the pressure upon the ordinary family to economize and the appeal to the struggling housewife made by the opportunity to save even a few cents on each purchase for the home. Besides, the public appetite for economy was especially keen at that time from the fact that the country was still in the grip of the financial panic of 1873. Any chance to buy cheaply was not to be overlooked.

His philosophy was simple: "*Show the American Housewife that she can save money by trading with you and you will win her patronage.* AND THE MORE EXCITEMENT AND COMPETITION YOU CAN PUT INTO HER SHOPPING THE BETTER SHE'LL LIKE IT."

This was about all that Mr. Lehmann saw when, in 1875, he opened up his little stock of jewelry, notions, crockery, hardware, and kitchen utensils. Later, he realized more and more that in the one word *Volume* lay the real secret of expansion. Volume in purchases would compel Volume in sales. Volume meant smaller profits but *more* profits. So he went out after *Volume.* Right here was the real foundation of the Department Store — and History is clear and definite in giving to Mr. E. J. Lehmann uncontested credit for founding the first Department Store. See Art and Literature of Business, Vol. I, by Charles Austin Bates.

THE FAIR IN 1915

The building in which this notable demonstration in centralized merchandising was sheltered was a little, one-story, frame structure that would to-day be called a shack. It contained only twelve hundred and eighty square feet of floor space and stood on the west side of State Street, just sixteen feet north of Adams. When it opened there was hardly a more insignificant store in that part of the city, but it was destined to do as much as any other enterprise, if not more, to make State Street the great permanent retail shopping thoroughfare that it is to-day. The whole investment made by Mr. Lehmann when he threw open his doors for the first day's business was less than a thousand dollars. Mark these two original figures: twelve hundred and eighty feet of floor space; one thousand dollars capital.

What extensions have forty years written in the expansion column opposite these entries? There is no secret as to the fact that Mr. Lehmann's great monument to the principle of down-town shopping contains 798,000 square feet of floor space and about eight miles of counters and show-cases. As to the investment, I can only conjecture that it is certainly high in the millions.

But let us get back to the little store from which this mighty volume of retail merchandising started and see what nourished a growth so marvelous.

There is more than a mere hint of the real secret of that success in the story of Mr. Lehmann's first sign. A few doors away, around the corner, was the paint shop of W. P. Nelson — whose sons have since become celebrated as interior decorators — and to this neighbor he explained that he was going to call his store "THE

FAIR" for two reasons: he wished to imply to those reading the sign that fair dealing would be given all customers and also that the store was like a fair because it offered many and different things for sale at a cheap price. The sign must not only proclaim the cheapness of the prices offered, but it must also be cheap itself, Mr. Lehmann added — and he must be permitted to pay for it a dollar at a time as he could spare it from his business. The bargain was struck and the sign painted. It read:

THE FAIR
CHEAP

This crisp sign, with its one descriptive word, pitched the key of the enterprise so clearly that he who ran might read. There was a flavor to the word "cheap" in those days of prolonged financial depression that caught the eye and stopped the feet of the passer. In just four years the "cheap" store had so expanded that it absorbed the shop in which the sign was painted — and paid for on the installment plan.

It had started with sixteen feet on State Street and, in four years, multiplied its total frontage by fourteen. How THE FAIR pushed out in every direction, absorbed one building after another and finally found itself "way 'round on Dearborn Street" is too long a chapter to be told in detail. But its growth may be suggested in a sentence: In an atmosphere of failure it thrived; as its neighbors shriveled and collapsed under the frost of financial depression, it expanded and eagerly took the room vacated by the outgoing enterprises.

WOMEN'S SUIT DEPARTMENT

The absorption of Sterns' Dollar Store is typical of many other passages in this period of THE FAIR's expansion.

By this time the merchant who had bought a "cheap" sign for a Cheap Store had turned over his stock so many times and had broken so many nickels in commerce with the common people that he felt a splendid faith in the new principle of Centralized Shopping and "plunged" to the extent of buying the entire stock of the Sterns store at the Sheriff's sale. This took no little courage, for it was a fifty-thousand-dollar stock.

In the meantime Mr. Lehmann had learned how to advertise. He found the mediums that reached the thrifty people who were counting their pennies, and he had learned how to tell his story so that these eager savers came down town to the great Central Shopping place to trade — because it was cheaper to do so.

In those days E. J. Lehmann deliberately ignored the trade of the rich and prosperous; he was too busy meeting the requirements of working people who wanted bargains and who were scrambling to save the pieces of the nickels that he broke for them, to pay attention to the demands of those who bought expensive articles and had not yet cultivated a consistent appetite for odd pennies.

Certainly these events made merchandising history with a sensational swiftness that contributed directly to two interesting results: making State Street the great permanent shopping thoroughfare — the Woman's Street of Chicago — and opening up to Chicago newspapers the immense possibilities of retail advertising and its revenue.

SILK DEPARTMENT

Certainly it is not too much to say that to-day many thousands of newspapers are bought solely to secure the shopping news, in the display pages of the great retail advertisers, instead of to get the general news of the world's happenings. In the field of retail advertising THE FAIR has been a pathfinder. As far as Chicago records show, it gave the newspapers their first double-page advertisement. This was on May 31st, 1885. Its advertising blazed the trail followed by almost the entire retail trade of the country. It did not hesitate to use sensational means to put its precedent-breaking campaign on its feet. Literally it sold silver dollars for ninety cents and five dollar gold pieces for $4.75. It taught the public "If you see it in an advertisement of THE FAIR, it's true" — and it is as resourceful and progressive to-day as it was under the personal generalship of the elder Lehmann. In connection with its thirty-sixth anniversary sale it used twenty pages of advertising display in each of two Chicago Sunday papers. Newspaper records show that THE FAIR has always been a pacemaker in advertising.

In those earlier days when THE FAIR absorbed the Marcus Sterns "Economy Block" and the James P. Dalton House Furnishing Store, everything was grist that came in its way. It literally swallowed the restaurant business of Alexander Brothers, installed it in a big church-like building decorated with large trees, palms, and a profusion of shrubs and vines and made this unique addition to its line a great attraction to the trade—a novelty feature at that time unknown to department store keeping.

In the art of buying Mr. Lehmann displayed the same unfailing genius for big merchandising that had made him the most talked of figure on State Street.

In 1885, at a sheriff's sale, he secured the stock of "The Famous" at a price that enabled THE FAIR to attract thousands of new customers to its counters. But it was later, in 1887, when Mr. Lehmann made his master stroke by securing at a court sale not only the entire stock of "The Bankrupt Store" but the lease of the store and its location.

It is one thing to handle the buying, the finances, and the organization of a store small enough to be supervised in all of its branches — almost in all of its details — by one man whose interest in its success is supreme; the test of a man's bigness comes when his business expands to proportions that compel him to become a general, trusting the details of buying, selling and accounting to others and devoting himself to a broad administrative oversight of the enterprise.

While the ideas of big buying, of big advertising, of "Everything for Everybody under one roof;" of retail merchandising for the millions; of down-town shopping for those that would save their pennies; of "Your money back if goods are unsatisfactory;" and of an almost unlimited variety from which to choose may not all have been definitely defined in E. J. Lehmann's mind when he hung out the sign "THE FAIR — Cheap;" they were there in the germ and came out naturally as the store developed.

In 1886 Mr. Lehmann had so greatly increased his business that he put his enterprise into the form of a corporation. A very convincing proof that the vision of this merchant included a department store in the complete sense of the term is found in the fact that whenever he was able to take on more space he added a new department instead of expanding an old one. He even rented space privileges to those who would put in new lines. Later, of course, he acquired these departments, as his financial strength increased. Always his aim appeared to be "Everything for Everybody under one roof."

Business grew by leaps and bounds in the latter Eighties and that period saw two changes of great importance: the capitalization was first increased, and the first store — the original one-story "shack"— was torn down and rebuilt to the height of three stories.

Even then the ultimate success of THE FAIR was so little realized that this building was considered a rather venturesome undertaking. But while it was still regarded as a novelty by the public, the management of THE FAIR realized that Down-Town trading would swamp them like a tidal wave if they did not speedily begin big constructive plans far greater than Mr. Lehmann had dared dream in the brightest days of his earlier successes.

Nothing short of a building containing the present great floor area would be sufficient to serve the demands of those who were certain to join the ranks of the down-town shoppers in the next few years. Therefore a quiet campaign for the securing of long-time leases was started —and was ended with success in time to allow the wrecking to start in the summer of 1890.

Instead of stopping business, the work of construction was so handled as to prove a valuable advertisement. To build a skyscraper about a great store without stopping business for an hour was then a greater novelty than it is now — but in the skill with which this problem was

MILLINERY DEPARTMENT

handled, THE FAIR maintained its reputation for the establishment of valuable precedents, for the working out of original ideas.

The great building was constructed in sections — practically in quarters — and on the completion of each unit the goods and counters were shifted between the usual closing hour of a Saturday night and the following Monday morning. The Dearborn Street half was finished in 1891 and the entire structure completed in 1896.

E. J. Lehmann, the founder of the enterprise, has been gone for many years — but THE FAIR, his Big Idea of "Everything for Everybody under one roof" at a cheap price, has never lost anything of the momentum that it gained under its founder. It has given a consistent example of acceleration, of steadily increasing progress. Under the sons of its founder it has maintained its record for the development of big retailing principles.

One of these later developments is the gaining of a new constituency without the weakening of the old source of support. Standards of living have changed greatly since the senior Lehmann put the word "cheap" underneath the name of his store on the sign that he hung on the front of his little "shack." And the most radical changes in those standards have taken place within the last few years when hardly a man who knew the store in its earlier stages has had a hand in its management.

The task of those in control of the destinies of THE FAIR in these later years has been that of advancing its policy to keep in step with those changing standards. Thousands of customers that traded at the little store on State Street, and at the larger store as the enterprise expanded, have become wealthy or at least prosperous. The mechanic of to-day enjoys an income and indulges in expenditures that were possible only to the successful business man of the Seventies and Eighties. Even the day laborer of the present enjoys comforts and luxuries that were not dreamed of in the pioneer period of the store's development.

THE FAIR has kept pace with this advancement of standard of living. It is still, as it always has been and undoubtedly always will be, the store of the people, the down-town shopping center for the Savers, the market place for the Thrifty. This policy is permanent; it was, so to speak, put into the corner stone of the first building and will always stand.

But will the family that formed the habit of trading at THE FAIR long ago, and that has become prosperous to the point of wealth, be obliged to go elsewhere in order to buy the things suited to its new estate — its enlarged fortunes? No.

To-day THE FAIR carries a satisfying selection of expensive goods, as well as the Cheapest of Everything — and everything between those two extremes.

Perhaps no point of policy has contributed more to the marvelous growth of THE FAIR than its rule that all articles must be exactly as advertised. The first task of the advertising manager is to see that this rule is not infringed. There is no way by which a department manager may more effectively invite trouble than to give the advertising manager a misleading and inaccurate description of an article. THE FAIR is keenly alive to the fact that the confidence of the buying public is the greatest asset of retail merchandising concerns.

Trustworthy merchandise must always be the running-mate of Honest Advertising, and this teamwork partnership is carefully maintained by THE FAIR. No transaction is considered closed by the mere exchange of the goods for the money called for on the price-ticket attached. The real close of the deal comes when the customer has found the goods to be satisfactory.

Still another point of policy that has done much to make this pioneer establishment in the field of Centralized Shopping the most popular of its kind is a systematic consideration for the convenience and the comfort of its customers. The branch Post Office, the quiet and inviting writing-room, the big general waiting room for men and women, and the nursery for mothers and babies; the free wrapping counters where customers may have their hand-parcels wrapped to suit their convenience and the check room where patrons may leave their bundles without charge are features that illustrate this attitude. In fact, the Credit Department is looked upon by the management as a convenience installed to serve the customers. Originally THE FAIR was strictly a cash store but the management finally became convinced that, as a matter of accommodation to customers, a credit department should be provided.

Light and air in unstinted quantities and the highest standard of cleanliness that can be maintained in a public place, frequented by thousands, are considerations of comfort not overlooked by THE FAIR. These sanitary provisions are appreciated alike by the customers and the employees.

Men's Furnishing Department

The attitude of THE FAIR towards its workers is suggested by its big Benevolent Association that has been consistently developed and encouraged by the management. This not only pays sick benefits to all employees who become ill, but also death benefits depending upon the salary that had been received by the employee involved. A visiting nurse is regularly employed to go to the homes of employees in case of sickness, and a physician is at the store to give free treatment to employees. The store hospital is, of course, the headquarters for the physician and nurses and is maintained to care for emergency cases among both customers and employees.

The Benevolent Association is not wholly concerned with the serious emergencies in the lives of employees. It aims to provide social entertainment as well as benefits. Its annual picnic for employees of THE FAIR and their families is an event that often calls together seven thousand persons. Probably the picnic is a bit distanced in a social sense by the Association's yearly ball. That of 1915 was held at the Hotel LaSalle. Throughout the season, the Benevolent Association gives several theatre parties. On these occasions the audience is composed entirely of employees of THE FAIR and their families and friends.

Just recall for a moment that E. J. Lehmann saw a vision of a great retail trade based on VOLUME. It is interesting to speculate upon what would have been his sensation if he could have seen with his own eyes the definition that his pioneer Department Store gave to this commercial world after he was gone.

Sporting Goods Department

Here are a few of the record purchases of THE FAIR that may give some idea of the magnitude of this store's buying transactions.

THE FAIR bought a shipment of twenty carloads of writing tablets—probably the largest single purchase of stationery ever made by a retail store. This seems to outclass even a shipment of twenty-two carloads of agate granite ware.

A single purchase of sporting goods made by THE FAIR is believed to have broken all retail purchase records in this line. It invoiced $127,000.00 and the transportation of this shipment—486 cases of goods—required 16 freight cars.

Still another purchase of unusual proportions was that of 4,950 trunks and about 35,000 bags and telescopes. The shipment of this great purchase of travelers' supplies required 17 freight cars of the largest type.

Of course the task of keeping up this mighty volume of incoming goods requires the services of a picked corps of men and women who are experts in their lines and who scour not only America but England, Scotland, Ireland, France, Austria, Switzerland, Germany and other foreign markets for merchandise.

But the meaning of Volume as that word to-day applies in the transactions of THE FAIR is not to be had wholly from the buying side of the business. The sales tell a wonderful story of achievement beyond anything dreamed of by the elder Lehmann when he laid the foundations of his enterprise.

When the bicycle was the real speed king, THE FAIR sold as many as one thousand of them in a single day.

Toy Department

What is far more remarkable, it recently sold one hundred motorcycles in one day.

In merchandise of an unusual sort the sales are often staggering in their extent. For example, in one season THE FAIR sold forty thousand dozen live frogs for bait. Also, this store disposes of more than twenty-thousand genuine Harz-Mountain singing canaries in a year. There is scarcely a novelty sold in this store that would not afford almost as startling statistics, on the score of volume, as these two live articles.

Turning to more staple articles, there is no trouble to find striking figures. A single day's sales of candy have reached the remarkable total of thirty thousand pounds.

THE FAIR's Grocery Department is one of the most complete of any in the world. Although size of stocks and variety of goods tell a somewhat graphic story, still, THE FAIR's Grocery Department is even more famous for its practical classifications of food products, for the cleanliness maintained and for the sanitary methods of handling groceries, meats, vegetables and other edibles. An idea of the size of this great Grocery section may be gathered from the fact that two million pounds of sugar and more than three million pounds of flour have been sold in one year.

The means required for the disbursement of goods also gives a vivid idea of the immensity of this store's trade. If all the motor and horse vehicles used by THE FAIR in the delivery of its goods were formed into a "circus parade," with the usual spaces between wagons, the caravan would be not less than two miles long. Delivery sub-stations are maintained in every

DELIVERY AUTOMOBILES

important section of the city. The most remote outposts of this sort are at Hammond, Indiana; and Highland Park, Elmhurst, Waukegan and La Grange, in Illinois.

Every device calculated to quicken the movement of goods after they have been sold, or to save labor in transferring them from one part of the store to another, has been provided. Much of the moving of heavy packages in the grocery department, for example, is done by means of mechanical conveyors. Then there are three kinds of vertical conveyors for delivering packages from the upper floors to the basement, where all outgoing merchandise is assembled and dispatched. Here, again, belt conveyors do much of the labor involved in distributing the packages into the cages that represent the various sections of the city. From these cages the goods are placed in trucks, elevated to the sidewalk and loaded into wagons and motor trucks for direct delivery or for forwarding to railway stations or delivery sub-stations.

How successfully THE FAIR has developed from its almost obscure beginning in that little sixteen-foot store on State Street, and how it has advanced the big idea of "Centralized Shopping," may be noted in the great number of different departments now flourishing under this one roof. At present these departments number almost one hundred, among which are stores devoted to

| | |
|---|---|
| Pictures and Picture Framing | Jewelry |
| Trunks and Suit Cases | Silverware |
| Baby Carriages | Watches and Clocks |
| Musical Instruments | Cutlery |
| Stationery and Office Supplies | Leather Goods |
| Printing and Engraving | Optical Goods |
| Toys and Dolls | Laces and Embroideries |

Veilings
Ladies Neckwear
Gloves
Silks and Dress Goods
Wash Goods
Hosiery
Ribbons
Umbrellas and Parasols
Artists' Materials
Fancy Goods
Linens
Handkerchiefs
Shoes
Groceries
Meats
Bakery Goods
Seeds and Bulbs
Cigars and Tobaccos
Kitchen Utensils
Hardware and Tools
Wooden and Willow Ware
Refrigerators
Stoves
Garden Implements
Lamps and Electroliers
Paints and Brushes
China
Glassware
Bric-a-Brac
Birds
Carpets and Rugs
Curtains
Bedding
Upholstery

Furniture
Underwear
Corsets
Women's Negligees
Infants' Wear
Men's and Boys' Furnishings
Men's and Boys' Clothing
Men's and Boys' Hats and Caps
Sporting Goods
Automobile Supplies
Camera Supplies
Harness and Horse Goods
Candies and Favors
Ice Cream and Soda Water
Women's Ready-to-Wear
      Apparel
Misses' and Children's
      Ready-to-Wear Apparel
Millinery
Notions
Sewing Machines
Dress Forms
Drug and Toilet Goods
Drug Sundries
Sheet Music
Books
Wall Paper
Hair Goods
Patterns
Religious Goods
Cut Flowers
Trusses
Restaurant
Photo Studio

as well as a broad selection of low-priced Merchandise
in the Bargain Basement.

Perhaps no array of figures can so vividly interpret
the full meaning of forty years of FAIR merchan-

dising as a few moments spent on the ground floor of this store watching the great human current move through the channel of the main aisle. Here is Volume beyond the wildest dream of the man who saw a vision of Centralized Shopping and its possibilities! Adams Street is hardly a more important thoroughfare between State and Dearborn Streets than is the great central aisle of THE FAIR.

There is hardly another point of vantage from which one may see so clearly that panorama of the marvelous changes in Chicago's "Down Town," scarcely another spot from which one may get so graphic a view of the great modern developments of retail trade as here where so much retail history has been made!

One cannot stand near the big State Street doors of this great establishment, watching the human tide that flows back and forth, without a vivid realization of the fact that THE FAIR is the People's Store. Young and old, rich and poor alike find their way through these hospitable doorways into the store that has been a friend to three generations of Chicagoans. Here everyone is welcome, whether buyer or visitor — here everyone is at home. The friendliness and hospitality with which the founder filled his first little shop have gone hand in hand with the growth of that shop to the great institution of to-day.

Here, on the corners of State, Adams and Dearborn Streets, this great monument stands as a full realization of the hopes and ambitions of him who founded this institution in a little, one-story, sixteen-foot store, just forty years ago.

CPSIA information can be obtained at www.ICGtesting.com
Printed in the USA
BVOW011012220413

318786BV00017B/547/P